T0368493

# A Heavenly Tea

Charlotte Waller with Jeannie Waller Zieren

WestBow Press books may be ordered through booksellers or by contacting:

WestBow Press
A Division of Thomas Nelson & Zondervan
1663 Liberty Drive
Bloomington, IN 47403
www.westbowpress.com
844-714-3454

Cover painting by Chase Quarterman
Special thanks to Jeannie Waller Zieren for editing and Bae Waller for photography.

ISBN: 979-8-3850-2609-8 (sc)
ISBN: 979-8-3850-2611-1 (hc)
ISBN: 979-8-3850-2610-4 (e)

Library of Congress Control Number: 2024910477

Print information available on the last page.

WestBow Press rev. date: 09/09/2024

WESTBOW
PRESS®
A DIVISION OF THOMAS NELSON
& ZONDERVAN

Dear Friends,

As God's people, we strive to bring honor and glory to Him in all that we do. One of the things that gives me great joy is bringing people together to share in "A Heavenly Tea". A Heavenly Tea glorifies God when He is our honored guest. God is honored as we lift our teacups as well as our hearts in prayer, fellowship, and love at all our tea parties.

My daughter, Jeannie, and I first worked on this book in 2008 and published it as a little booklet to share with family and friends. Now, in 2024, we have given the book an updated look for anyone who loves tea parties and wants to share about Jesus.

I hope you enjoy this book, but most of all I pray that you may experience the incomparable joy of knowing Jesus Christ as your personal Lord and Savior. To Him be all the Glory!

Love,
Charlotte

# I. Scripture

*The heavens declare the glory of God; the skies proclaim the work of his hands.* Psalm 19:1 (NIV)

God shows Himself in innumerable ways. Just as He displays His Glory in the heavens, He also displays and receives glory in simple things like sweet fellowship with other believers over a cup of tea. To have tea, all you need is fresh water, a tea kettle, a cup, and saucer, and of course, tea. *A Heavenly Tea* acknowledges the presence of the Lord and considers the objects of a tea as symbolic of our relationship to our Heavenly Father.

**Teacups** represent people. Like a teacup, every person is unique and made in God's image. All of us have chips and cracks and stains because we are all sinful and imperfect. But God, in His love and grace, sees us as His beautiful and redeemed children perfected by His Son's sacrifice on the cross.

*For you created my inmost being; You knit me together in my mother's womb. I praise You because I am fearfully and wonderfully made; Your works are wonderful; I know that full well.* Psalm 139:13-14 (NIV)

The **Tea Pot** represents God. God wants to fill us with His Holy Spirit just as a tea pot pours into a teacup. Praise God every morning and ask Him to replenish you with His love.

In this life, there are many choices to make regarding how you spend your time, money, and energy. Make sure to fill your life with God first. Satan, our enemy, will try to distract you by keeping you so busy that you have little time left to spend with the Lord. Experience the freedom in making the Lord your sole pursuit, and the other things in life will flow from your wellspring of love that comes from Him.

*Open your mouth wide and I will fill it.* Psalm 81:10b (NKJV)

*But the fruit of the Spirit is love, joy, peace, longsuffering, kindness, goodness, faithfulness, gentleness, and self-control.* Galatians 5:22-23a (NKJV)

**Sugar Cubes** represent the sweetness of growing in Jesus. Reading and studying the Bible, prayer and journaling, fellowship with other believers, and being involved in a church body will be the light on the path where God leads you. Fill your life with "sweet" things that bring pleasure to God and to your soul.

*Taste and see that the Lord is good; blessed is the one who takes refuge in Him.* Psalm 34:8 (NIV)

*Call to me and I will answer you and tell you great and unsearchable things you do not know.* Jeremiah 33:3 (NIV)

*You come to the help of those who gladly do right, who remember your ways.* Isaiah 64:5a (NIV)

**Cream** represents the choices we make. Each day, you decide what to fill your cup with—who you spend time with, what you eat and drink, where you go and what you do, what you watch and read, and where you spend your time and money. God will bless your life and those around you when you consider Him in the choices you make each day.

*Choose for yourselves this day whom you will serve.* Joshua 24:15a (NIV)

*Take your everyday, ordinary life—your sleeping, eating, going-to-work, and walking-around life—and place it before God as an offering.* Romans 12:1-2 (The Message)

A **Lemon** represents the sour choices we make or the misfortunes that happen during our lives because we live in a fallen world.

*For all have sinned and fall short of the glory of God.* Romans 3:23a (NIV)

Remember the old saying, "When life gives you lemons, make lemonade?" Sometimes, we allow anger then bitterness to seep into our hearts over the things that have gone wrong in our lives because we are only human. But as Christ followers, we are given a divine understanding to choose right from wrong and in the way we respond. God's Word promises to fill us with a peace that passes all understanding when we cast our burdens on the Lord. He also promises to never leave us or forsake us.

*In this world you will have trouble. But take heart! I have overcome the world.* John 16:33b (NIV)

A **Rose** (or any flower) in a vase on the tea table represents our spiritual growth as Christians when we abide with Him and remain rooted in His love. A rose receives its beauty, sweet aroma, and vitality from its source—water. We also draw nourishment from the Living Water, our Lord Jesus Christ, as we read His word, pray, and worship Him daily.

*If you declare with your mouth, "Jesus is Lord," and believe in your heart that God raised him from the dead, you will be saved. For it is with your heart that you believe and are justified, and it is with your mouth that you profess your faith and are saved.* Romans 10:9-10 (NIV)

*I am the vine; you are the branches. If you remain in me and I in you, you will bear much fruit; apart from me you can do nothing.* John 15:5 (NIV)

A **White Tablecloth** (or white tea napkin) represents purity. Jesus was perfect and lived a sinless life, but He willingly took our place and gave up His life for us on the cross. When we repent and turn from our sins, His blood cleanses us from all sin and removes the stain of guilt and shame. When we believe that Jesus died for us, He covers our sin and imperfections with His own righteousness. We can never be right with God on our own, but His covering washes and redeems us, and we can now stand holy and unblemished before God and have a personal relationship with Him.

*Jesus answered, "I am the way and the truth and the life. No one comes to the Father except through me."* John 14:6 (NIV)

*Cleanse me with hyssop, and I will be clean; wash me, and I will be whiter than snow.* Psalm 51:7 (NIV)

A **Tea Tray** represents our firm foundation in Jesus Christ as our Savior and Lord. Believe that Jesus is your personal Savior and commit to following Him all the days of your life. He is the only sure foundation for this life, and He is our full assurance of eternal life in heaven.

*For God so loved the world that he gave his one and only Son, that whoever believes in him shall not perish but have eternal life.* John 3:16 (NIV)

We have the power in Jesus to choose whether sin will enslave us in this lifetime or whether we will live victoriously knowing the battle is the Lord's and not ours to fight. Living victoriously means keeping our eyes fixed on Him and believing that God will reap a harvest from our pain and sorrow. The journey of following Christ is not easy, and the road of suffering may seem long, but the ultimate battle has already been won. Victory is His, and as children of God, it is also ours to claim!

*He who was seated on the throne said, "I am making everything new!"* Revelation 21:5a (NIV)

When life disappoints, keep your eyes focused on God, and He will see you through the hard times. Each day is a new day to commit to Him, and He promises to renew our hearts and minds as we draw near to Him. Enjoy the sweetness and the warmth of God's love and presence by filling your cup fresh with Him each day. He will replenish your strength once again!

Remember, *the heavens declare the glory of God; the skies proclaim the work of his hands* (Psalm 19:1a, NIV). Consider the vastness and beauty of the sky that He made and contemplate your own small insignificance. Yet God created you to play a very important part in the history of His people. Use what you've been given and live for Him! May your cup overflow with the renewal of His love and grace every day.

*I will lift up my eyes to the hills—from whence comes my help? My help comes from the Lord, who made heaven and earth.* Psalm 121:1-2 (NKJV)

# II. Design & Decor

A little preparation goes a long way in hosting a tea party. Be ready for your guests rather than running around with last minute preparations (like I have been known to do, ha!). Preparation will ensure your own peace of mind as well as provide a welcoming scene for your guests. As my military husband tells me, "Leave yourself a margin of time," so you are prepared for any unexpected events or little emergencies (or if you have a guest arrive early!). Also, try to do as much as you can ahead of time, so you are not completely worn out by the time your guests arrive. You want to enjoy the tea party, too!

## *One Day Before the Tea*

- Have your teapots, teacups, plates, and trays washed and dried and ready to use.
- Polish any silver that you may use.
- Set the table(s) with tablecloth(s), teapots, teacups, small plates, stirring spoons,
- small spreading knives, and cloth or delicate paper napkins. You may also want to set out glasses for water.
- Make any sandwiches that can be wrapped in plastic and keep in the refrigerator (For recipes and preparation, see Section IV).

**Helpful hint**: Cover finger sandwiches with damp paper towels to preserve moisture and seal with plastic wrap in container.

- Place paper or crochet doilies on serving trays (two and three-tiered trays are lovely).
- Decorate the room with any other items appropriate for the tea party occasion. For a traditional afternoon tea, fresh flowers are sufficient. A dress-up tea party would call for vintage gowns, hats, fur stoles, gloves, and other clothing items to be hung around the room or placed over the backs of chairs for guests to wear (and makes for great pictures!). For more decorating ideas for theme parties, see Section V.

## The Morning of the Tea

- Finish setting the table with silverware and silver or glass pieces.
- Pick up fresh flowers or pick flowers from your garden for the centerpiece.

**Helpful Hint:** Place spray roses or other small flowers in small bud vases around the tea table (these are charming and inexpensive).

- Arrange centerpiece and set candles around for a late afternoon or garden tea.
- Make any last-minute recipes (such as scones and chocolate-dipped strawberries).
- Wash and pat dry any garnish you will be using (such as parsley for tomato or cucumber sandwiches and mint leaves for iced water).
- Slice lemons and cover with plastic wrap.
- Fill sugar bowls with white and/or brown sugar cubes. Have packets of a sugar substitute available.
- Be sure you have enough serviettes for each guest.
- Fill teakettle with fresh, cold water ready to boil. For a larger tea, fill a hot water carafe and plug it in.

## 30 Minutes Before Tea

- Heat water and bring to a boil.
- Place sliced lemons on serving tray and pour cream into cream pitcher.
- Fill silver ice bucket with ice cubes and silver or glass pitchers with water.
- Add ice and pour water into glasses just before guests arrive.
- Spoon scone toppings into serving tray: your choice of jelly, Devonshire cream, and lemon curd.
- Choose tea flavor and steep a few tea bags or loose tea (according to size of teapot) for 3-5 minutes.

- For larger teas, you can also set out a box of individual tea packets for guests to choose from and then fill up their cups at the hot water carafe.
- Serve tea as soon as guests sit down.
- Play soft tea music (hymns of praise on the piano are perfect).

House all ready for tea guests.

# III. Presentation

Teatime is like a small meal, so a blessing is always appropriate. This is also an ideal time to share God's message of love and salvation with the items set up for the tea. I like to have an extra tea setting on a tray to illustrate as I share the symbolic meaning of each tea item.

**Pour tea.** Tell guests the flavor of tea you are pouring (Earl Grey, Lady Grey, English Breakfast, Darjeeling, etc.). I love to start with a flavorful black tea such as Lady Grey (a lighter version of the traditional Earl Grey) followed by a peach tea, or another black tea infused with fruit flavor.

Try several kinds before and serve your favorites (or the favorite of your guest of honor!). You may also need to fill glasses of water in case a guest does not care for tea. Pass the serving tray around with cream (or milk), sugar and slices of lemon. Make guests aware that mixing cream and lemon together will curdle and make buttermilk!

**Serve tea sandwiches.** These should be dainty "finger-size" sandwiches with crusts trimmed off. For a pleasing visual display, cut sandwiches in a variety of shapes: squares, triangles, circles, or theme-appropriate shapes (such as hearts for Valentine's Day or trees for Christmas). Sandwiches can be open-faced or closed. You should have at least one type of sandwich for each guest to try on the tray. When the tray is empty, refill and serve again. You may also leave the tray with remaining sandwiches on the table after serving guests the first time.

**Helpful hint:** Depending on the number of guests, you may need extra help with serving. You may also choose to let guests pass the tray around and help themselves. If you prefer to serve, pause between each pair of chairs. This allows two people to serve themselves from each side of the tray.

**Serve more tea.** Offer a bowl or dish for guests to pour cold tea out when offering a new flavor of tea.

**Serve scones.** Scones, or sweet biscuits, are available in a variety of flavors to buy or make (raisin, chocolate chip, blueberry, cinnamon, etc.). Tell guests what kinds you are serving. Circulate the serving tray with jelly, lemon curd and Devonshire cream (or heavy whipped topping). Tell guests to try a dab of each by spooning a small dallop on their plates. The guests can then use their own knives to spread the jellies and creams on their scones.

**Helpful hint:** For a beautiful tray, go for an array of color, such as Devonshire cream, lemon curd, and strawberry or blackberry jam (see Recipes in Section IV).

**Serve more tea.** Serve more tea or a different flavor of tea if you like.

**Serve desserts.** Dessert consists of small bites of something sweet. Encourage guests to try one of everything. Good choices that are bound to please the eyes and palate are lemon and chess squares, Symphony brownie bites, and chocolate-dipped strawberries (see Recipes in Section IV).

**Serve more tea.** You may also need to pour more iced water.

# IV. Recipes

## First Course: Tea Sandwiches

Afternoon tea sandwiches are made from thinly sliced bread with crusts removed. Spread bread slices with unsalted butter, herb butter, mayonnaise, or cream cheese. Add filling and cut into desired shapes. For open-faced sandwiches, top with a garnish for a perfect finishing touch.

**Helpful hint:** Use cookie cutters to make precise shapes, especially for holiday or themed parties.

Tea sandwiches may be made ahead of time and covered with a damp towel or plastic wrap and refrigerated until serving time. Decorate trays with crochet, linen or paper doilies, fresh flowers, or herbs in bud vases.

## Ground Chicken Sandwiches

2 cups ground chicken
¾ cup mayonnaise
1 T. lemon juice
Salt and pepper to taste
Bread rounds (or banana muffins, see below)
Capers, drained

Boil chicken breasts, remove bone and skin, and put through grinder or food processor. Mix with mayonnaise and seasonings. Spread on firm bread rounds and garnish with capers. Makes about 3 dozen.

**Helpful hint:** To save time, buy your favorite brand of chicken salad from your local grocer or deli and spread on bread rounds.

# Banana Nut Bread (or Muffins)

3 cups all-purpose flour
2 cups sugar
1 tsp. baking soda
1 tsp. salt
1 tsp. cinnamon
1 cup chopped nuts (optional)
3 eggs, beaten
1 ½ cups oil
2 cups mashed ripe bananas
1 8 oz. can crushed pineapple
2 tsp. vanilla

Combine dry ingredients; stir in nuts and set aside. Combine remaining ingredients and add to dry mixture, stirring just until batter is moist. Spoon batter into greased and floured 9 x 5 x 3-inch loaf pans. Bake at 350 degrees for one hour or until done. Cool for 10 minutes in pan. Freezes well.

Also makes great mini muffins. Bake for about 12-15 minutes. Eating chicken salad on banana nut bread or muffins is always a favorite!

# Cucumber Sandwiches

2 (3 oz.) pkg cream cheese
6 T. sour cream
2 T. garlic salad dressing mix (Good Seasons)
2 cucumbers, scored and thinly sliced
1 dozen stuffed green olives, sliced (optional)
4 dozen cocktail rye bread slices

Soften cream cheese in a bowl. Add sour cream and salad dressing mix. Stir to blend. Spread on rye bread slices and top with a slice of cucumber and a slice of olive.

## Tomato Sandwiches

2 (3 oz.) pkg cream cheese
6 T. sour cream
2 T. garlic salad dressing mix (Good Seasons)
6 tomatoes, scored and thinly sliced
1 T. rosemary, chopped fine
4 dozen white bread rounds

Soften cream cheese in a bowl. Add sour cream and salad dressing mix. Stir to blend. Spread on round slices and top with a sprinkle of rosemary garnish.

## Cream Cheese, Celery and Walnut Sandwiches

¼ lb. cream cheese, room temperature
Parsley sprigs (for garnish)
White or whole wheat bread
¼ celery heart, very finely chopped
¼ cup diced walnuts

In a small bowl, beat cream cheese until smooth. Mix in celery and walnuts. Make sandwiches with cream cheese mixture. Trim off crusts and cut sandwiches into rectangles or triangles. Garnish plate with sprigs of parsley.

## Pimento and Cheese

Grate 1 lb. of hoop cheese
1 small can pimento
Dash of garlic powder
Loaf of rye cocktail bread
Dash of Worcestershire
1 cup of mayonnaise (more if needed to make a creamy spread)
Top rye slices with pimento slice for garnish

**Helpful Hint**: To save time, buy your favorite brand of pimento and cheese spread from your local grocer or deli and spread on bread rounds.

## Second Course: Scones and Toppings

Scones are quite simple to make. However, a packaged scone mix can also deliver good results. You can add extras to scones depending on you and your guests' tastes. Try cut-up apples, currants, cinnamon, apricots, fresh blueberries, cranberries, walnuts or even chocolate chips.

## Basic Scones

2 cups flour
1 T. baking powder
6 T. butter
Lightly beaten eggs
2 T. sugar
½ tsp. salt
½ cup buttermilk

Mix dry ingredients. Cut in 6 T. butter until mixture resembles coarse cornmeal. Make a well in the center of batter and pour in buttermilk. If you don't have buttermilk, use regular milk. Mix until dough clings together and is a bit sticky—do not over-mix. Turn out dough onto a floured surface and shape into a 6-to 8-inch round, about 1 ½ inches thick. Quickly cut into pie wedges or use a round biscuit cutter to cut circles. The secret of tender scones is a minimum of handling. Place on ungreased cookie sheet, being sure the sides of the scones don't touch each other. Brush with egg for a shiny, beautiful brown scone. Bake at 425° for 10 to 20 minutes or until light brown.

**Helpful hint**: For a sweet treat, soak sugar cubes in orange juice for less than a minute then press into top of warm, plain scone. To save time, buy small tea-sized biscuits and add cinnamon and sugar on top.

## Mock Devonshire Cream

Real Devonshire cream is a very rich, sweet cream made in England. However, this "mock" Devonshire cream recipe is quite good.

½ cup heavy cream or 8 oz. softened cream cheese
2 T. confectioners' sugar
½ cup sour cream

In a chilled bowl, beat cream until medium-stiff peaks form, adding sugar during the last minutes of beating. (If you are using cream cheese, just stir together with sugar.) Fold in sour cream and blend. Makes 1½ cups.

# Lemon Curd

Lemon curd, sometimes called lemon cheese, is a very common English preserve. It is used as a spread for sandwiches, muffins, crumpets, and so forth, and it also makes a delicious tart filling.

Grated peel of 4 lemons
4 eggs, beaten
½ cup butter, cut into small pieces
2 cups sugar
Juice of 4 lemons (about 1 cup)

In the top of a large double boiler, combine lemon peel, lemon juice, eggs, butter, and sugar. Place over simmering water and stir until sugar is dissolved. Continue to cook, stirring occasionally, until thickened and smooth. While hot, pour into hot, sterilized ½-pint canning jars, leaving about ⅛-inch for headspace. Run a narrow spatula down between lemon curd and side of jar to release air. Top with sterilized lids; firmly screw on bands. Place in a draft-free area to cool and store in a cool, dry place (or the refrigerator). Lemon curd doesn't keep indefinitely, so make only as much as you will use in a couple of weeks. Makes about 1 pint.

Helpful hint: You can also purchase lemon curd at specialty grocery stores.

## History of Tea

According to ancient legend, a Chinese emperor discovered tea in 28th century B.C. The emperor boiled his drinking water for health reasons. One time when he did this, an evergreen leaf fell into his water. He sipped the water without knowing, and he loved the taste! News spread quickly in the kingdom about the emperor's invention, and soon everyone was gathering evergreen leaves to put into their water. Thus, tea became part of the Chinese culture. It was not long before other civilizations caught onto the concept of drinking tea.

Tea reached English shores around 1660. Anna, seventh Duchess of Bedford (1783-1857), is thought to have originated the "afternoon tea." In England, people were accustomed to eating late dinners when the men got back from hunting. Ladies, like Anna, would experience "sinking spells" around 3:00 p.m. when waiting for the men to return. Anna began taking tea in the afternoon, and the trend soon caught on with all the noblewomen.

The English people's love for tea was instilled in the colonists who settled in America. Tea is very important to American history. In fact, it is taught in all American history books. The Boston Tea Party was a political statement of action by American revolutionists who defied the British control of imports to the colonies by dumping expensive shipments of tea into the Boston harbor. The history and tradition of tea is important to people of many cultures around the world.

## Symphony Brownie Bites

½ cup margarine
1 cup sugar
4 eggs
1 cup flour
½ cup nuts, chopped
1 can Hershey chocolate syrup
Add 3 large Symphony candy bars if not using frosting

Cream margarine and eggs. Mix flour and sugar. Blend rest of ingredients. Spread half of mixture in a greased 9 x 13 casserole dish. Layer three Symphony bars and top with remaining mixture. Bake at 350 degrees for 20-25 minutes.

Optional Frosting: Make first to let cool and thicken. 5 T. milk, 6 T. margarine, 1½ cups sugar, 1 tsp. vanilla. As it cools, it hardens. Spread on cooled brownies.

Helpful Hint: To save time, use your favorite brownie mix and divide the batter in half and place chocolate bars in the middle of layers before baking.

## Sand Tart Cookies

1 cup butter, softened
½ cup powdered sugar
2 tsp. vanilla
2 cups flour
2 cups nuts, chopped
½ tsp. salt

Cream butter and powdered sugar. Stir in vanilla, salt, and flour; mix well. Stir in nuts. Shape into small balls. Bake on ungreased cookie sheet at 325 degrees for 20-25 minutes. Roll in powdered sugar after baking or put powdered sugar in plastic bag and shake gently.

## Lemon Squares

2 sticks butter
½ cup powdered sugar
2 cups self-rising flour
2 cups sugar
Rind of lemon, grated

Topping:
4 eggs beaten
½ tsp. baking powder
6 T. fresh lemon juice
¼ cup flour
pinch of salt

Cream butter, sugar, and flour. Pat into bottom of well-greased pan (9 x 13). Bake 20 minutes at 350 degrees. Add topping. Mix all ingredients and pour over baked crust. Bake at 350 degrees for 20-25 minutes. Sprinkle while warm with powdered sugar if desired and wait until cool to cut. Add more lemon juice for more tartness. Best if made 24 hours before serving. Freezes well. Makes 48 squares.

## Easy and Delicious Chess Squares

1 stick oleo, melted
1 box yellow cake mix
1 beaten egg

Mix and spread on the bottom of an oblong greased casserole or cookie sheet with sides.

Top with a mixture of the following:

1 8 oz. pkg. cream cheese
1 box sifted confectioners' sugar
3 eggs
½ tsp. vanilla

Bake at 350 degrees for 25 minutes. Cut into small squares when cool.

## Chocolate-dipped Strawberries

Wash and dry one-pint (or more depending on number of guests) of strawberries. Melt chocolate bark and stir to make smooth. Dip strawberries into warm chocolate and lay on wax paper to harden. Keep in a cool, dry place until time to serve.

# V. Themes

All teatimes, whether a tea for one or a large group tea, can be done in a heavenly way and promote joyful fellowship with the Lord and special friends. Teas are also perfect occasions to share the love of the Lord in a relaxed environment. A tea party is a time to love, encourage, and get to know or catch up with each another. We give thanks with a blessing at each of these tea parties and share God's love through the meaning of the tea items. Enjoying teatime can be a heavenly experience—a little taste of heaven right here on earth! Any activity, when used as a ministry for the Lord, brings Him pleasure. Just as the taste of tea and friendship warms the inside, so the joy of the Lord should fill our hearts.

*For the joy of the Lord is our strength.* Nehemiah 8:10b (NIV)

## Small Teas

## Just for You Tea

For any time during the day. Great with a quiet time or devotional in the morning, a break-time during the workday, or a calm-down time with herbal tea in the evening before bed.

*Draw near to God, and He will draw near to you.* James 4:8a (NKJV)

## Tea for Two

For you and one other special person; husband, brother, sister, neighbor, child, grandmother, or friend. Celebrating a birthday, new friend in town, or for just a time to chat is reason enough!

*For the entire law is fulfilled in keeping this one command: 'Love your neighbor as yourself.'* Galatians 5:14 (NIV)

## "Praying Hands" Tea Basket

Pack a "tea to go" and visit a friend in the hospital, nursing home or someone homebound.

*For God has said, 'I will never leave you, I will never forsake you.* Hebrews 13:5b (NIV)

## Picnic Tea

Pack a basket for tea, including a thermos of hot water, tea bags and Styrofoam cups. Take to a lake, park, the beach, or even just the backyard or porch.

*He leads me beside quiet waters.* Psalm 23:2b (NIV)

## Teatime at the Office

Pack a tea for break-time at the office. Take extra tea and a sweet treat for coworkers.

*Each of you should use whatever gift you have received to serve others.* I Peter 4:10a (NIV)

## Larger Teas

Larger teas are often held outside the home in a more spacious but less charming setting (like a church fellowship hall). A larger room can be transformed into tea party enchantment with the right details. Small vases (even unused teapots) of fresh flowers and candles are a nice touch as well as fresh rose petals scattered across white tablecloths. An easy and effective centerpiece is a hat stand with a vintage hat placed on top. Dress up chairs with yards of tulle tied in big bows at the back. Use old lace to top off white tablecloths whenever possible. And arrange for a church pianist and other talented musicians (flutist, harpist, vocalist) to entertain with classic hymns or soft praise music.

## Bible Study Tea

A Bible Study Tea can serve to kick off a new Bible Study and may include previewing the new bible study book and meeting new and old friends. Along with tea and food, Bible verses and books are placed on tables.

*If you abide in My Word, you are my disciples indeed: And you shall know the truth, and the truth shall make you free.* John 8:31b-32 (NKJV)

**Helpful Hint:** Instead of name cards, use printed Bible verses (theme verses for the Bible study) as place settings. Or place bookmarks of encouraging scripture on trays with food.

## Bridal Tea or Bridesmaids' Tea

Adorn table with small figurines of brides and grooms. Place a whimsical veil on the back of the bride's chair and take pictures with her wearing it. A bridal decoration I treasure is a wicker mannequin dressed in a vintage bridal dress and veil I found at a flea market. The mannequin stands outside the front door for guests to see as they walk in.

*For from Him and through Him and for Him are all things. To Him be the glory forever! Amen.*
Romans 11:36 (NIV)

## Mother-to-Be Tea

For this charming tea party, use baby and stork figurines on the table and baby bonnets. If you know the gender of the baby, decorate accordingly in soft pinks or blues.

*This is what the Lord says—He who made you, who formed you in the womb, and who will help you.* Isaiah 44:2a (NIV)

**Helpful Hint:** Coordinate the centerpiece of the table with the theme of the party. For example, a silver, three-tiered tray can display the delicate trinkets appropriate for the theme of the party. A sweet gesture for the guest of honor is displaying pictures of the honoree and using these pictures as decoration. Prop pictures against bud vases or place in small tea frames on table.

## Graduation Tea

This tea is a perfect party for a senior graduating from high school or college. Use student's graduation picture and decorate with her school colors.

*'For I know the plans I have for you,' declares the Lord, 'plans to prosper you and not to harm you, plans to give you a hope and a future.'* Jeremiah 29:11 (NIV)

## Holiday Tea

Most any holiday is a worthy occasion to host a tea party. Some of my favorite holiday teas are a Mother's Day Tea, a Valentine's Day Tea for widows, and a "Happy Birthday Jesus" Christmas Tea for children. Use holiday cups, saucers, and teapots.

*Do not forget to entertain strangers, for by so doing some have unwittingly entertained angels.*
Hebrews 13:2 (NKJV)

Children's Christmas Tea

## Healthy Tea

This one is very near and dear to my heart. I have enjoyed having my exercise class to my home for tea over the years. You can serve a "healthy" version of the traditional afternoon tea. For a larger group, testimony and song make the event inspiring and uplifting.

*Do you not know that your body is a temple of the Holy Spirit, who is in you, whom you received from God? You are not your own; you were bought with a price. Therefore honor God with your bodies.* 1 Corinthians 6:19-20 (NIV)

**Helpful Hint:** Suggestions for a delicious and healthy tea: serve green, herbal, or decaffeinated tea.

- First course: turkey, tomato or cucumber slices on thin wheat bread and pimento and cheese on celery sticks.
- Second course: blueberry scones with reduced-fat pancake mix served with fat-free or light whipped topping, lemon curd made with honey (instead of sugar), and sugar-free jam or jelly.
- Third course: desserts could be any low-calorie cakes, and of course, strawberries dipped in dark chocolate. Fresh fruit speared on toothpicks is delicious like grapes, pineapples, and kiwi.

## Neighborhood Tea

Enjoy the neighborhood nostalgia of years past and invite neighbors to walk over to your house for a cup of tea and something sweet to eat. Arrange the tea buffet-style with pick-up food and a hot water silver urn with several choices of tea bags. As a fun conversation starter, ask each neighbor to bring his or her own special teacup and saucer to use. Let each one share why this teacup is special to them.

## Garden (or Porch Tea)

Place roses or any other garden flowers in teapots, watering cans or on a hanging basket. (If it happens to be an evening tea, be sure and light a few candles for a very special touch.) Use old quilts or vintage tablecloths to make a lovely setting.

*'I am the true vine, and my father is the gardener.'* John 15:1 (NIV)

## Birthday Tea

A Birthday Tea is for anyone, ages 4 to 104! Be sure and have a glittery crown for the birthday girl to wear or a special hat with bright feathers, flowers, etc. For children, use child-sized teacups. Birthdays are great occasions to get dolled up. Hats, pearls, brooches, gloves, fur, and lace really make the party a hit.

*Love the Lord your God with all your heart and with all your soul and with all your mind and with all your strength.* Mark 12:30 (NIV)

## Children's Tea

These parties are my favorite! For "tea", make pink lemonade. Peanut butter and jelly sandwiches or turkey sandwiches, sugar cookies (for children to ice and decorate with colored sprinkles), baked goldfish snacks, and a birthday cake are my staple food items. I like to top the cake with a miniature tea set for the birthday girl to keep. Fun activities include "stations" where guests can make bead bracelets, put on make-up (or have older girls put it on), paint their fingernails, and style their hair.

*'Let the little children come to Me, and do not forbid them; for of such is the kingdom of God.'* Mark 10:14b (NKJV)

For boys, a "Cowboy Tea" is a big hit. Decorations include red and white bandanas, speckled blue cups and teapot, cowboy hats and boots, rope, and any Western toys. Relay races, horseshoes, and piñatas are fun outdoor games.

*And Jesus took the children in His arms, placed his hands on them and blessed them.* Mark 10:16 (NIV)

**Helpful Hint:** Never use your finest china or anything you would care if it were to break. Remember, kids are kids!

## Mother-Daughter Tea (Extend to grandmothers, aunts, or special women in your life.)

Perfect for all ages! Also great as a women's event at church. This is a wonderful time to be thankful for your loved ones.

*Teach them to your children, talking about them when you sit at home and when you walk along the road, when you lie down and when you get up.* Deuteronomy 11:19 (NIV)

*Children are a heritage of the Lord.* Psalm 127:3a (NIV)

## Drinking From My Saucer

I've never made a fortune,
And it's probably too late now.
But I don't worry about that much,
I'm happy anyhow.

And as I go along life's way,
I'm reaping better than I sowed.
I'm drinking from my saucer,
'Cause my cup has overflowed.

Haven't got a lot of riches,
And sometimes the going's tough.
But I've got loving ones around me,
and that makes me rich enough.

I thank God for his blessings,
and the mercies He's bestowed.
I'm drinking from my saucer,
'Cause my cup has overflowed.

O, Remember times when things went wrong.
My faith wore somewhat thin.
But all at once the dark clouds broke,
And sun peeped through again.

So Lord, help me not to gripe,
About the tough rows that I've hoed.
I'm drinking from my saucer,
'Cause my cup has overflowed.

If God gives me strength and courage,
When the way grows steep and rough.
I'll not ask for other blessings,
I'm already blessed enough.

And may I never be too busy,
To help others bear their loads.
Then I'll keep drinking from my saucer,
'Cause my cup has overflowed.

Jimmy Dean

# About the Author

Charlotte B. Waller was born in Corinth, Mississippi. She grew up in Biggersville, a small community seven miles south of Corinth. The eldest of three and only daughter, Charlotte grew up watching her mother, grandmothers and several aunts cook, clean, and entertain with the generous hospitality and charm inherent of strong, gracious Southern women.

It is no wonder then that entertaining and hospitality came naturally to the petite brunette. As a little girl, Charlotte was whisked out of the kitchen by the older women cooking and handed a feather duster to clean with. She still admits that she is foremost a housekeeper before a cook, but she found a perfect match of light baking and preparation in tea party hosting. With a love for hospitality and other people, Charlotte fell in love with tea parties. Charlotte uses her education degree to encourage tea drinkers—ages four to 104—and her enthusiasm for life (college cheerleading and 40+ years teaching exercise at church) to host fun and meaningful tea parties in her home, church, and other venues.

For Charlotte, this small ministry is foremost an outlet to serve the Lord. She uses tea parties to share God's love and goodness. The Lord equips His people with different gifts, talents, and abilities to build His kingdom, reach the lost and give glory to His name. Charlotte trusts the Lord to lead her and views her tea ministry as a call to service. Whether in word or deed—through music, dance, crafts, sports, and yes, even tea parties—all can give praise to God. To God be the Glory for the great things He has done!

# A Love for Tea Parties

When asked where her love for tea parties came from, Charlotte remembers a very special woman in her growing up years, her grandmother Ardena M. Honnoll. "Othermama" would allow Charlotte to serve tea and cake at her church's circle meetings and made it seem a special privilege for Charlotte to serve the older ladies. Othermama was a living example of a gracious hostess, a wise grandmother, and an affectionate friend to Charlotte, and she lived a long and fruitful life of 91 years.

Other women served as role models to Charlotte as she began to realize the gifts and abilities the Lord had given her. She remembers going to a birthday tea party for Jane, her next-door neighbor and childhood friend. Miss Nina, Jane's mother, held a tea party in her home for Jane's ninth birthday, and the young girls felt so grown up and ladylike with their paper-made hats and cups of tea. As she grew, there were several more friends, young and old, who ministered to Charlotte with a cup of tea and encouraging conversation. Some of these women were mentors who took an interest in Charlotte when she first moved to the "big city" of Jackson to teach school as a young single.

In Jackson, Charlotte found a church home at First Baptist Church, located in the heart of downtown. The converted Presbyterian girl met Bill Waller Jr., a young Jackson attorney, through the singles' ministry at the church. Bill admired Charlotte's legacy of hospitality—he started calling her after she had him over to eat some of Othermama's deviled eggs and leftovers! In marriage, Bill encouraged Charlotte in her hospitality endeavors, but as young parents, the couple's primary duty was raising William, born in 1980, Jeannie, born in 1982 and Clayton, born in 1991. As parents, Bill and Charlotte instilled a love for the Lord in their three children, who asked Jesus in their hearts at young ages.

Charlotte's memories of participating and hosting tea parties date back to giving Jeannie a tea party for her fourth birthday. With the help of teenage babysitters in the neighborhood, Charlotte created "salon stations" in her home for Jeannie and her preschool friends. The girls were decked out in high heels, dresses, hats, and pearls and had their hair, make-up and nails done. Jeannie's favorite great-aunt, Joy O. Holmes, sketched portraits of the young children. There were also fun games and activities for the good-natured boys who came to play. The party was a hit, and Jeannie had several more tea parties as she grew up—one at 10, 16 and even 21 with college friends' home for the holidays.

Aunt Joy's portrait of Jeannie at her four-year-old tea party

As Charlotte's children grew older, Bill's three brothers and Charlotte's two brothers got married and started their own families. Charlotte feels blessed to count 11 nieces and 5 nephews in her family, most who live within a few miles of each other. To show her love as an aunt, Charlotte decided to host a birthday tea party for each one when they turned four. With encouragement and decorating ideas from her artist friend Lisa Baker, who liked to "tie things up with a bow," Charlotte learned how to transform a room into a delightful children's tea party. Even the boys had a cowboy themed tea party. The tea parties were held in Charlotte's open-air carport and backyard with a long table and child-sized china. The nieces and nephews loved it, and Charlotte offered to host a more grown-up tea party for the nieces when they turned 10 and invite a special friend or two. All the older nieces have also been given a high school graduation tea. Charlotte has also enjoyed giving her granddaughter, Ella Charlotte, a five-year-old birthday tea.

By word-of-mouth, Charlotte began to host tea parties for friends' children at her home and church. Cups, saucers, dessert plates and more items for the larger tea parties were found at thrift stores or donated by older women in the church. Charlotte has enjoyed speaking at other church's teas for women's events over the years. Proceeds from teas are donated to a local ministry of choice.

The Lord has shown Charlotte many avenues for her tea party ministry. "A Heavenly Tea" has served to promote fitness and health as a "Heavenly Healthy Tea" as well as church staff teas, bridal and baby shower teas, children's birthday teas, senior citizens' teas, "Happy Birthday Jesus" teas, women's bible study kick-off teas, and more.

While the occasions for tea parties may differ, each party is designed in the same manner with coordinating scripture, design and decorations, recipes, music, and tea of course. It is Charlotte's prayer that each party reflects the True Giver of every blessing and God's everlasting kindness and goodness.

*Taste and see that the Lord is good!* Psalm 34:8a (NIV)

Use these pages to save special photos of the tea parties you have with family, friends, neighbors, and special people the Lord brings along your path.

<Insert 4x4 space for photo>

<Insert 4x4 space for photo>

&lt;Insert 4x3 space for photo&gt;

&lt;Insert 4x3 space for photo&gt;

Printed in the United States
by Baker & Taylor Publisher Services